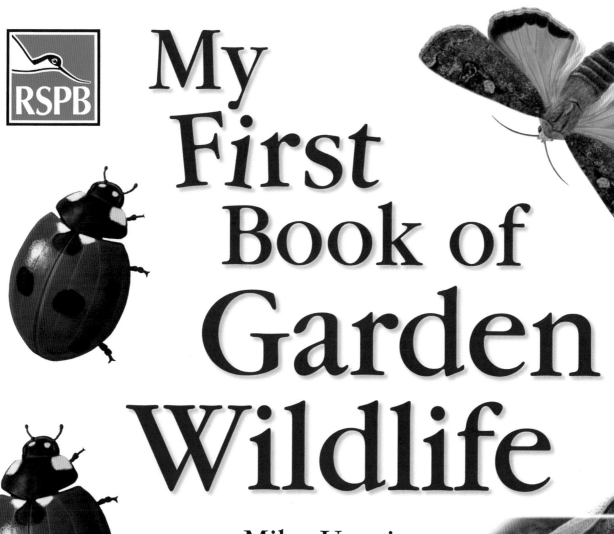

My First Book of Garden Wildlife

Mike Unwin

Illustrated by
Tony Sanchez

A & C BLACK • LONDON

Published 2008 by A & C Black Publishers Limited
36 Soho Square, London W1D 3QY
www.acblack.com

ISBN: 978-1-4081-0457-6

Printed and bound in Milan by Rotolito

A & C Black uses paper produced from elemental chlorine-free pulp,
harvested from managed sustainable forests.

Also in this series:
RSPB My First Book of Garden Birds by Sarah Whittley and Mike Unwin,
illustrated by Rachel Lockwood

Original concept for **My First Book of Garden Birds** by Rachel Lockwood and Sarah Whittley

To see our full range of books
visit www.acblack.com

Contents

Wildlife in your garden

Every garden can be a good home for wildlife. More creatures will visit your garden if you give them the things they need. Ask a grown-up for help.

All wildlife needs food. A little overgrown corner provides animals with seeds, insects and other food all year round. Keep feeders topped up for birds and leave out some old fruit in winter.

All animals need a home. Thick bushes make good nesting places for birds. A rockery offers a home to frogs and toads. A tree hole might even hide a bat.

Water is important, too. A pond makes a home for all sorts of wildlife, while a birdbath offers a drink to many thirsty animals.

Are you ready to meet some garden wildlife? Read the clues on each Guess who! page to see if you can work out which animal is hiding there.

Then find the answer by turning the page.

Be a nature detective

It's not always easy working out who lives in your garden. Here are some clues to look out for.

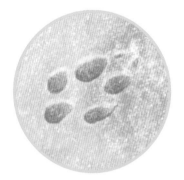

Paw prints show that someone has been walking about.

A bright eye shows that someone is hiding in a hole.

Nibbled fruits and berries show that someone has been tucking into a meal.

Guess who!

Look! Paw prints in the snow.
You have a secret visitor in
your garden.

Do you see that bushy tail?
Look closer, before it disappears.

Can you tell who it is?

A fox

Your secret visitor is a fox.

That thick coat keeps her warm and snug, even on the coldest winter nights. Her long ears listen for danger and her shiny black nose sniffs out food.

It's hard to find enough to eat in winter. With luck, she might catch a mouse or two.

Guess who!

These old apples from autumn are all bruised and rotten.

But someone must be enjoying them. They've pecked lots of holes.

There are footprints, too.

Who can it be?

A blackbird

It's a blackbird. Look at his shiny yellow beak. Peck, peck, peck. Yum!

That brown bird waiting her turn is a female blackbird.

Blackbirds love to eat juicy worms, but these are hard to find when the ground is frozen. Old fruit makes a tasty treat that lasts until spring.

Guess who!

Yellow and purple, orange and white: crocuses are sprouting up all over.

Spring must be on the way.

But why is that flower shaking about? And what's that funny noise?

Bzzzzzzzz...

A bumblebee

The spring sunshine has woken up a bumblebee. It had been fast asleep under some leaves since autumn. Now it is visiting flowers to sip their sweet nectar.

Those yellow lumps on its furry legs are pollen. This comes from inside the flower.

The bumblebee carries pollen from one flower to the next. It helps new flowers to grow.

Guess who!

What's that bubbly jelly floating in the pond?
It's full of little black specks.

Look closer. Something is hiding underneath
it. Something green. Something with long
legs and BIG feet.

What can it be?

A frog

It's a frog. Those long legs are for jumping and those big feet are for swimming.

The jelly is called frogspawn. It is made of hundreds of frogs' eggs stuck together. The black specks are tiny tadpoles, ready to hatch.

Guess who!

Gulp, gulp, gulp! Somebody's having a drink.

This big bird must be thirsty. It doesn't take small sips like other birds, but sucks up the water through its beak — just like drinking through a straw.

Look at those colours: pink, green, purple and a splash of white.

Do you know who it is?

A woodpigeon

Woodpigeons are big birds. They waddle around, puffing out their chests, and often visit water for a long drink.

You can tell them from other pigeons by their smart white collars.

You can often see a male and female sitting side by side. Listen out for their gentle cooing calls.

Guess who!

Plants are bursting into life all over the garden. Look at the new buds and fresh, green leaves.

But look closer. Are they all leaves?

Or can you see someone hiding?

17

A butterfly

A flash of yellow! It's a brimstone, the first butterfly of spring.

It looked just like a leaf when its wings were folded. Not even hungry birds could spot it.

But now it swoops and flutters around the garden, as bright as a daffodil.

Guess who!

Something's scurrying along the wall, gathering moss.

It sticks its beak into every nook and cranny. It's small and brown, like a mouse, but it's covered in feathers.

Who is it?

19

A wren

It's a wren. You can see his pointy beak and sticky-up tail.

This busy little bird builds his nest in a hidden hole. He uses moss, leaves and grass to make it strong and snug.

A male may make more than five nests. But a female chooses just one of them. Then she lines it with soft feathers and lays her eggs inside.

Guess who!

Many different creatures find food and shelter on the wall.

One has left a sticky, slimy trail.

Follow the trail. You might find out who made it.

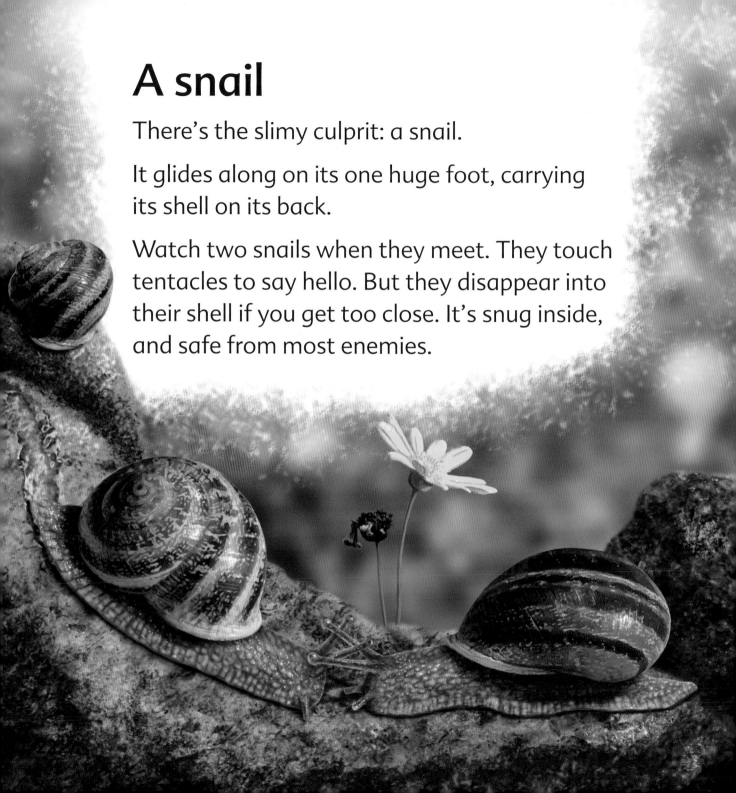

A snail

There's the slimy culprit: a snail.

It glides along on its one huge foot, carrying its shell on its back.

Watch two snails when they meet. They touch tentacles to say hello. But they disappear into their shell if you get too close. It's snug inside, and safe from most enemies.

Guess who!

Now something's watching you.

It's hiding under that rock. Can you see its beady golden eye?

Who can it be?

A toad

Aha! A big fat toad.

Its skin is drier and lumpier than a frog's.
And females, like this one, are bigger than males.

Toads hide away in cool, shady places, then pop out
at night for a bite to eat. A juicy worm makes a tasty
meal. One more gulp and down it goes.

Guess who!

Look out, toad! Better get back under your rock. Here comes something that might swallow you up.

It's slithering silently through the grass, flicking its forked tongue in and out.

But what is it?

A grass snake

It's a grass snake. Stand still! This beautiful reptile is very shy. It will quickly disappear if you move.

Don't worry. It's not poisonous. But it swallows frogs and toads whole.

Grass snakes often lay their eggs in compost heaps, where they are warm and hidden from view.

Guess who!

Snuffle, sniffle, grunt. Something is shuffling around the flowerbed.

Do you see that twitchy nose?

Shhh! Here it comes.

Who can it be?

27

A hedgehog

It's a hedgehog, searching for slugs, worms and snails.

At the first sign of danger it rolls up into a spiky ball. Don't touch! Those spines are sharp.

Look out for hedgehogs at night, especially after rain. Try leaving out a little cat food in a saucer. It makes a tasty change from slugs.

Guess who!

What's that? Something's sitting tight on that branch.

Look closer. It has folded wings with a pattern that looks just like bark.

What can it be?

A moth

Surprise! You've disturbed a large yellow underwing moth. It flashes its bright yellow back wings as it flies away to safety.

Most moths come out after dark. They sip nectar from flowers and lay their eggs in secret places.

Guess who!

Something else is fluttering around in the dark.

It's too big to be a moth. But it's not a bird either. It chases insects in crazy circles around the treetops.

What can it be?

A bat

It's a furry bat. Her wings are made of stretchy skin spread out between long fingers.

By day, bats rest in a hidden hole in a tree or building. They fold their wings and hang upside down by their feet.

At night, bats come out to chase moths and other insects. They catch their food in mid-air.

Guess who!

Cheep, cheep, cheep!

These baby birds are hungry. They open their beaks wide to beg for food. Yesterday they left their nest. But they still don't have their grown-up feathers.

Whose babies are they?

33

A blue tit

Here comes their mother. She's a blue tit. See her pretty yellow, green and blue feathers.

Soon her babies will have these colours too. But first they need plenty of food to help their new feathers grow.

The mother stuffs caterpillars into the babies' hungry mouths. In a few days the babies will learn to feed themselves.

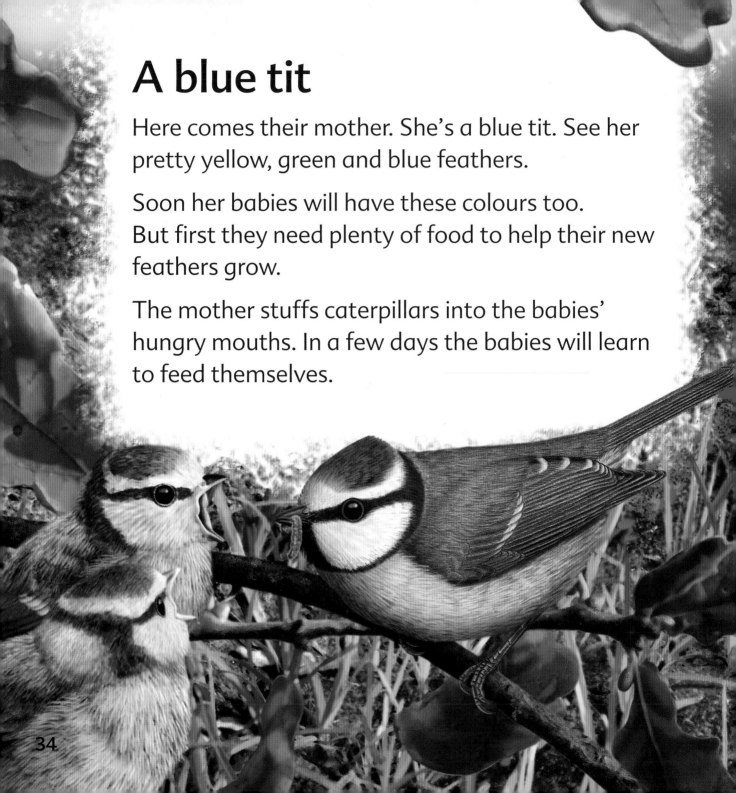

Guess who!

Cough, splutter!
Who's kicking up all that dust?

Chirp, chirp, chirrup!
They sound like birds.

But what are they?

35

House sparrows

They are house sparrows. That one with the black bib is a male. The other one is a female.

Sparrows love to bathe in dry, dusty soil. It may look dirty but it helps to clean their feathers.

A dry summer's day is perfect. They stretch out their wings and spread the dust all over. Look out for the little hollows they make in flowerbeds.

Guess who!

Nibble, nibble, nibble.
See those tiny tooth marks?

Somebody has been nibbling the strawberries.
Somebody with a long tail.

Who can it be?

A house mouse

It's a house mouse. Mice can live in houses and gardens. They dig little burrows and build nests of grass inside.

Those sharp little teeth nibble all sorts of things. Fruit, nuts and seeds. Sometimes even worms.

Look out. They might nibble your food, too.

Guess who!

Somebody is hiding in this rose bush.

Take a close look at the thorny stem.
Can you see tiny legs?

There must be something on the other side.

But who can it be?

Ladybirds

Those legs belong to ladybirds. These colourful little beetles often land on rose bushes. Gardeners love ladybirds because they eat greenflies.

Their bright colours are a warning to birds. They say: "Leave me alone. I taste horrible!"

Some ladybirds have only two spots. Others have more.

Guess who!

Glittering dewdrops show where a web is hanging.

Look at the neat pattern. Gently tap the sticky strands of silk with a blade of grass. Be careful not to break them: this web belongs to somebody.

Do you know who?

A garden spider

A garden spider built this web. Look at its fat body and pretty white markings. This one is a female. She is much bigger than a male.

When an insect flies into the web, it sticks. The spider dashes out to wrap her prey in more silk. Then she carries her meal to the edge of the web and gobbles it up.

Guess who!

Autumn leaves are turning red, orange and brown. They're falling all over the lawn.

But somebody is too busy digging to notice. Somebody with a big, fluffy tail.

Who can it be?

3

A grey squirrel

This grey squirrel is busy storing away nuts and acorns. It buries some of them in the lawn and hides others in secret tree holes.

In winter, squirrels remember where they hid food and come back to dig it up again. Their hidden supplies can last until spring.

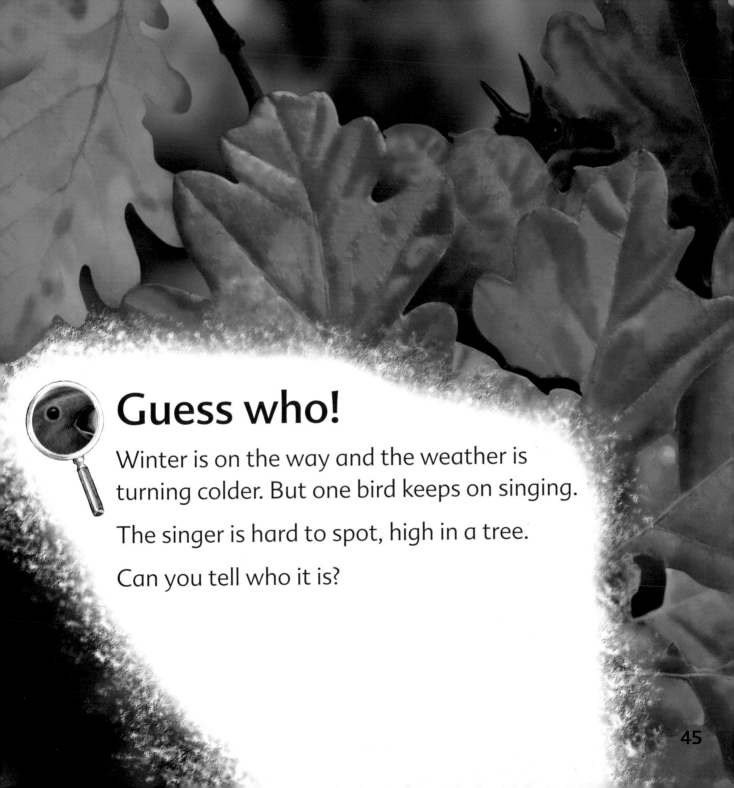

Guess who!

Winter is on the way and the weather is turning colder. But one bird keeps on singing.

The singer is hard to spot, high in a tree.

Can you tell who it is?

A robin

It's a robin. Now you can see the bright red breast.

This little bird sings all year long. Sometimes even at night.

His song tells other male robins that the garden belongs to him. In spring, a female robin will join him and together they will build a nest.

Wildlife words

burrow   underground home for an animal

cooing   gentle noise made by pigeons and doves

culprit   guilty person (or animal)

feeder   hanging container full of seeds or nuts for birds

pollen   tiny, dusty grains that a flower produces to help it make seeds

nectar   sugary liquid produced by plants that attracts insects

compost   rotting garden waste, such as cuttings and lawn trimmings

greenflies   tiny green insects that cause damage to some plants

markings   patterns on an animal

Find out more

If you have enjoyed this book and would like to find out more about garden wildlife, you might like RSPB Wildlife Explorers.

Visit **www.rspb.org.uk/youth** to find lots of things to make and do, and to play brilliant wildlife games.

Index